Collins

SNAP REVISION
FORCES & ELECTRICITY

GW00750568

SNAP
REVISION
FORCES &
ELECTRICITY

OCR Gateway GCSE Physics

OCR
GATEWAY
GCSE
PHYSICS

REVISE TRICKY
TOPICS IN A SNAP

Contents

Published by Collins
An imprint of HarperCollinsPublishers
1 London Bridge Street,
London, SE1 9GF

© HarperCollins*Publishers* Limited 2016

9780008218140

First published 2016

10 9 8 7 6 5 4 3 2 1

British Library Cataloguing in Publication Data.

A CIP record of this book is available from the British Library.

Printed in United Kingdom by Martins the Printers

ACKNOWLEDGEMENTS

The author and publisher are grateful to the copyright holders for permission to use quoted materials and images.

Every effort has been made to trace copyright holders and obtain their permission for the use of copyright material. The author and publisher will gladly receive information enabling them to rectify any error or omission in subsequent editions. All facts are correct at time of going to press.

HT Higher Tier content

How To Use This Book

To get the most out of this revision guide, just work your way through the book in the order it is presented.

This is how it works:

Revise
Clear and concise revision notes help you get to grips with the topic

Revise
Key Points and Key Words explain the important information you need to know

Revise
A Quick Test at the end of every topic is a great way to check your understanding

Practise
Practice questions for each topic reinforce the revision content you have covered

Review
The Review section is a chance to revisit the topic to improve your recall in the exam

Electric Charge

You must be able to:

- Recall that in everyday objects there are many atoms, each with electrons
- Recall that friction can transfer some electrons from one object to another, so that both objects become charged
- Understand that electric current in metal conductors, including wires, is a result of the flow of large numbers of electrons
- Understand that resistance to current produces heat, which transfers energy from the circuit to the surroundings.

(Electricity)

Electric Force and Electric Charge

- Electric force can be attractive or repulsive and can act at a distance.
- Electric force acts between bodies that have net charge.
- There are two types of charge – positive and negative.
- When many charged particles, such as electrons, move together they form an electric current.
- In a neutral atom, the negative charge of the electrons is balanced by the positive charge of the nucleus.
- The unit of charge is the coulomb (C).

Key Point

Electric force holds atoms together. It is the dominant force between individual atoms and between the nuclei of atoms and electrons.

Electrostatic Phenomena

- Forces between objects much larger than atoms can be observed when there is an imbalance of positive and negative charge.
- The observations, or phenomena, are called static electricity, or electrostatics, because the charged particles are not flowing.
- Friction can transfer electrons from one object to another:
  - one object will have an excess of electrons and a negative charge
  - the other object will have a shortage of electrons and a positive charge.
- The space around a charged object is called its electric field.

Key Point

All electrons are the same. They are extremely small and they all have the same negative charge.

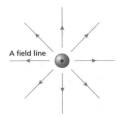

Electric Field Lines Around a Single Positive Charge

A field line

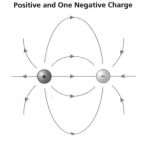

Electric Field Lines Around One Positive and One Negative Charge

The arrows show the direction of the force that can act on a small positive charge in different places.

Sparks

- A very strong electric field can cause particles of air to separate into electrons and 'atoms' with a shortage of electrons.
- These charged 'atoms' are positive ions.
- The electric field can accelerate the charged particles.
- When there is a lot of movement of charge between the objects, the air sparks.

Electric Current

- Metals are conductors of electricity.
- When many electrons move in the same direction in a wire, there is an electric current.
- Electric current inside a closed loop of wire can be continuous if the electrons experience continuous force from a source of energy.
- Batteries and cells, for example, can create continuous force.
- Ammeters are used to measure current.
- They are connected into circuits so that the circuit current flows through them.
- Current is measured in amperes or amps (A).
- Current is equal to rate of flow of charge:

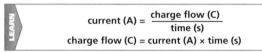

$$\text{current (A)} = \frac{\text{charge flow (C)}}{\text{time (s)}}$$
$$\text{charge flow (C)} = \text{current (A)} \times \text{time (s)}$$

- Unless it is isolated (cut off) from other objects, a conductor cannot keep excess electric charge, because electrons flow in or out of it too easily.

Resistance

- Current can flow through an electrical conductor, such as a metal wire, but there is always some resistance to the flow.
- This resistance means that a wire can be heated by an electrical current. Energy passes from the wire to the surroundings.
- Resistance is measured in ohms (Ω).

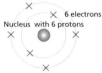

A Neutral Atom

6 electrons
Nucleus with 6 protons

A Positive Ion

5 electrons
Nucleus with 6 protons

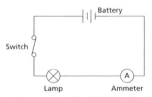

Battery
Switch
Lamp
Ammeter
A

For a current to flow in this circuit there must be an energy supply and a complete loop (or closed circuit).

Key Words

electric current
neutral
phenomenon
electrostatics
transfer
electric field
ion
conductor
battery
cell
ammeter
resistance

Quick Test

1. What are the two types of electric force?
2. a) Outline how an object, such as an inflated balloon, becomes electrically charged.
   b) Explain why it is **not** possible to charge a metal spoon in the same way as the balloon.
3. What is the difference between charge and current?
4. Describe how resistance causes transfer of energy from a circuit.

Circuits

You must be able to:

- Understand that resistance to current produces heat, which transfers energy from the circuit to the surroundings
- Understand that a potential difference, or voltage, is needed to keep a current going around a circuit
- Investigate the relationship between current and voltage for different components.

Electricity

Circuits and Symbols

- A system of symbols is used to represent the different components in circuits.
- The components in electrical circuits can be connected in series or in parallel (see pages 8–9)

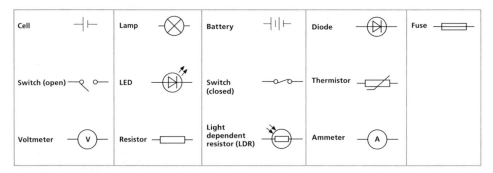

Potential Difference or Voltage

- Batteries and other power supplies can replace the energy that is transferred out of the wires and components in a circuit.
- Batteries and other power supplies only work when they are part of a circuit.
- A battery has a positive terminal (which attracts negative charge, so it attracts electrons) and a negative terminal (which repels negative charge).
- The abilities of batteries or other power supplies to provide energy to moving charge in a circuit can be compared using potential difference or voltage.
- Potential difference or voltage is measured in volts (V).

LEARN energy transferred (J) = charge (C) × potential difference (V)

- Voltmeters are used to measure voltage.
- A voltmeter is connected to two points. The circuit current does not flow through a voltmeter.

Key Point

For continuous current, a continuous potential difference and a continuous loop of conductor (such as wire and other components) are necessary.

Key Point

The potential difference between two points in a circuit is 1V if 1J of energy is transferred when 1C of charge passes between the points.

Revise

A voltmeter measures a difference between two points in a circuit.

Current, Potential Difference and Resistance

- An increase in potential difference can increase the current in a circuit.
- An increase in resistance in a circuit can decrease the current.

$$\text{current (A)} = \frac{\text{potential difference (V)}}{\text{resistance (}\Omega\text{)}}$$

potential difference (V) = current (A) × resistance (Ω)

Current–Voltage Relationships

- If the temperature of a metal wire doesn't change, its resistance doesn't change.
  - Current is proportional to voltage.
  - A current–voltage (I–V) graph is a straight line that passes through the origin of the graph.
  - The relationship between current and voltage is linear.
- For a wire that gets hotter as voltage and current get bigger, the resistance increases and the relationship between current and voltage is non-linear.
- This happens in a filament lamp, in which the wire is white hot.
- A thermistor behaves in the opposite way to a wire.
- As it becomes hotter, more electrons become free to move, so its resistance goes down.
- For a thermistor the current–voltage relationship is also non-linear.
- Thermistors are sensitive to changes in temperature.
- This means thermistors can be used as electrical temperature sensors.
- Diodes and Light Dependent Resistors (LDRs) also have non-linear current–voltage relationships.
- Diodes only allow current in one direction. When a voltage is in the 'reverse' direction, no current flows.
- For LDRs, when the light intensity increases, the resistance goes down.

Wire with Little Heating

A Wire That Gets Hot at a Higher Voltage (e.g. A Filament Lamp)

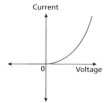

Diode (Reverse Voltage Produces Zero Current)

Quick Test

1. Explain why a voltmeter is connected to two points in a circuit that are separated by a component, such as a resistor.
2. Outline what can cause the current in a simple circuit to a) increase and b) decrease.
3. Explain why a current–voltage graph for a wire becomes curved when the wire becomes hot.
4. What happens to the resistance of a thermistor when its temperature increases?

Key Words

component
series
parallel
positive terminal
negative terminal
potential difference
voltage
voltmeter
origin
thermistor
sensor
diode
light dependent resistor (LDR)

Electricity: Revise
7

Resistors and Energy Transfers

You must be able to:

- Calculate the resistance of two or more resistors in series or in parallel
- Understand that resistors transfer energy out of circuits by heating and motors are used to transfer energy out of circuits by doing work
- Recall that rate of transfer of energy is power
- Perform calculations on power, energy, voltage, current and time for use of electricity by appliances at home.

Resistors in Series

- Resistors can be connected in **series** – one after the other.
- Since both resistors resist current, their total resistance is greater than their individual resistance.
- Total resistance is the sum of the individual resistances:

total resistance (R_t) = resistance 1 (R_1) + resistance 2 (R_2)

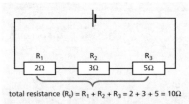

total resistance (R_t) = $R_1 + R_2 + R_3$ = 2 + 3 + 5 = 10Ω

- The current in each of the resistors must be the same.
- Current is flow and, if there is only one route for it to flow along, it must be the same at all points.

potential difference (V) = current (A) × resistance (Ω)

- If the current is the same in two resistors but the resistances are different, the voltages must be different.
- The relative size of the voltages is the same as the relative size of the resistances.

$$\frac{\text{voltage 1 } (V_1)}{\text{voltage 2 } (V_2)} = \frac{\text{resistance 1 } (R_1)}{\text{resistance 2 } (R_2)}$$

Resistors in Parallel

- Resistors can be connected in **parallel** – one alongside the other.
- This gives current two routes to follow, so the total resistance is smaller than either of the resistors:

$$\frac{1}{\text{total resistance } (R_t)} = \frac{1}{\text{resistance 1} (R_1)} + \frac{1}{\text{resistance 2} (R_2)}$$

Key Point

When two resistors are in series, current must pass through both of them.

- Resistors in parallel have the same voltage.
- If the resistances of two resistors in parallel are different:
  - they do not carry the same current
  - the current will be larger in the smaller resistor.

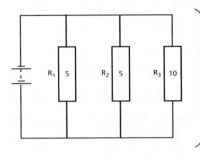

$$\frac{1}{R_t} = \frac{1}{R_1} + \frac{1}{R_2} + \frac{1}{R_3}$$

$$= \frac{1}{5} + \frac{1}{5} + \frac{1}{10}$$

$$= \frac{5}{10}$$

$$R_t = \frac{10}{5} = 2\Omega$$

Transfer of Energy

- Current in resistors heats them. Thermal energy is transferred.
- Motors also transfer energy. They do that by exerting force that can make objects move – they do work.
- Motors are not designed to provide heat, but they do transfer some energy by heating their surroundings.

Electrical Power

- The rate at which a component in a circuit transfers energy is its power, measured in watts (W) or kilowatts (kW).
- Since power is rate of transfer of energy:

> **LEARN**
>
> $$power = \frac{energy\ transferred}{time}$$

- Energy can be measured in joules (J), kilojoules (kJ) and kilowatt-hours (kWh).
- In circuits, power is related to current and voltage:

> **LEARN**
>
> **power (W) = potential difference (V) × current (A)**
> **= (current (A))² × resistance (Ω)**

Quick Test

1. Calculate the total resistance of a 2Ω resistor and a 4Ω resistor when they are connected a) in series and b) in parallel.
2. Describe how motors transfer energy out of a circuit.
3. A resistor has a current of 1.5A and a potential difference of 12V.
   a) Calculate how much heat energy it transfers to its surroundings in 60 seconds.
   b) What is the power of the resistor?

Practice Questions

Electric Charge

1 What must a body have to experience an electric force?

    A positive charge   **C** either positive or negative charge

    B negative charge   **D** positive and negative charge   [1]

2 Why can an object, such as a balloon, become charged when rubbed?

    A friction creates electrons

    B friction destroys electrons

    C friction transfers electrons

    D friction gives electrons extra charge   [1]

3 What is produced by the movement of many electrons in the same direction?

    A an electric charge   **B** an electric current   **C** an electric resistance   [1]

4 What is the unit of resistance?

    A amp   **B** coulomb   **C** ohm   **D** volt   [1]

5 Electric force can be attractive or repulsive.

    a) What does that tell us about electric charge?   [1]

    b) Sketch two charged bodies attracting each other and show their charge.   [1]

    c) Sketch two charged bodies repelling each other and show their charge.   [1]

6 Explain why:

    a) metals are good at conducting electricity   [1]

    b) a resistor gets hot when the current is large   [2]

    c) resistance is smaller when two resistors are in parallel than when there is only
        one of them.   [1]

Total Marks _____ / 11

Circuits

1. What voltage is needed to drive a 2.5A current through a 20Ω resistor?

   A 8V   **B** 20V   **C** 22.5V   **D** 50V   [1]

2. Which of these statements is correct?

   A The relationship between current and voltage in a wire is always linear.

   B The relationship between current and voltage in a wire is linear provided the wire does not get hot.

   C The relationship between current and voltage in a wire is always non-linear.

   D The relationship between current and voltage in a wire is non-linear provided the wire does not get hot.   [1]

3. Which of these diagrams shows the correct connection of an ammeter and a voltmeter?   [1]

   A

   B

   C
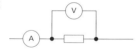

   D
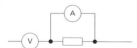

4. How does a resistor transfer energy to its surroundings?

   A heating   **C** storing energy

   B doing work   **D** creating energy   [1]

5. At what rate does a resistor transfer energy if it carries a current of 0.5A and is connected to a voltage of 1.5V?

   A 0.75W   **B** 1.0W   **C** 2.0W   **D** 3W   [1]

Practice Questions

6 What is the SI unit of energy in electric circuits?

    A amp   **B** joule   **C** volt   **D** watt   [1]

7 Which of these equations is **not** correct?

    A charge moved = current × time

    B potential difference = current × resistance

    C energy transferred = power × time

    D resistance = current × potential difference   [1]

8 Explain the problem, if any, with each of these circuits.

a)   [1]

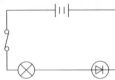

b)   [1]

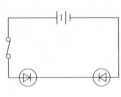

c)   [1]

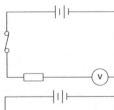

d)   [1]

9 Explain what each of the following components are used for.

    a) battery or cell   [1]

    b) ammeter   [1]

    c) voltmeter   [1]

    d) resistor   [1]

    e) diode   [1]

    f) thermistor   [2]

    g) LDR   [2]

10 A current of 1.5A passes through a 6Ω resistor. Calculate:

    a) the voltage   [3]

    b) the amount of charge that flows through the resistor in 60 seconds   [3]

    c) the energy transferred by the resistor in 60 seconds   [3]

    d) the rate of energy transfer.   [3]

Total Marks _____ / 32

Resistors and Energy Transfers

1 Which of these circuits has the least resistance? (All of the resistors are identical.)

A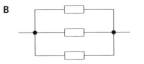

C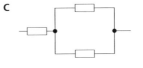

B

D  [1]

Total Marks _____ / 1

Forces

Journeys

You must be able to:

- Make measurements and calculations of speed, time and distance
- Calculate the kinetic energy of a moving body
- Understand the importance of vector quantities (displacement, velocity and acceleration) when considering motion
- Interpret displacement–time and velocity–time graphs
- Calculate acceleration.

Speed and Velocity

- Miles per hour (mph) can be used to measure the speed of vehicles.
- However, in the standard international SI system, metres per second (m/s) is used.
- 1m/s is equal to 3.6 kilometres per hour (km/h or kph) and 2.24mph.
- Distance and speed are scalar quantities (without direction).
- They are used when direction is not important.
- When thinking about energy, direction is not important.
- The energy of a moving body is called kinetic energy, which is measured in joules (J).

> **kinetic energy (J) = 0.5 × mass (kg) × (speed (m/s))²**

- This equation can be used for predicting journeys:

> **distance travelled (m) = speed (m/s) × time (s)**

- When direction is important, displacement and velocity are used.
- Quantities with direction are vector quantities.
- Arrows of different lengths and directions can be used to compare different displacements and different velocities.
- A negative vector quantity means it is in the reverse direction.

$$\text{velocity} = \frac{\text{displacement}}{\text{time}}$$

Key Point

You must be able to rearrange the distance equation to work out speed and time, i.e.

$$\text{speed} = \frac{\text{distance}}{\text{time}}$$

$$\text{time} = \frac{\text{distance}}{\text{speed}}$$

If the speed on a journey varies, the average speed is given by the total distance divided by the total time.

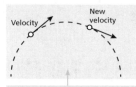

An object moving in a curved path with constant speed has a changing velocity, because the direction of motion is changing.

Graphs of Journeys

- Displacement–time graphs can be used to describe journeys.
- The slope or gradient of a displacement–time graph is equal to velocity.

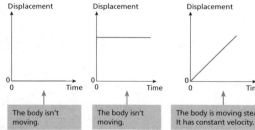

The body isn't moving.

The body isn't moving.

The body is moving steadily. It has constant velocity.

Velocity is increasing. The body is accelerating.

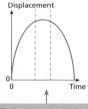

The body turns around and returns to where it started.

- Velocity–time graphs can be used to describe the same journeys.

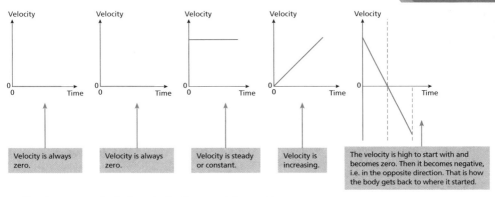

| Velocity is always zero. | Velocity is always zero. | Velocity is steady or constant. | Velocity is increasing. | The velocity is high to start with and becomes zero. Then it becomes negative, i.e. in the opposite direction. That is how the body gets back to where it started. |

- The slope or gradient of a velocity–time graph is equal to acceleration.
- HT The enclosed area under a velocity–time graph is equal to displacement.

Acceleration

- Acceleration is rate of change of velocity. It is a vector quantity.

LEARN

$$\text{acceleration (m/s}^2) = \frac{\text{change in velocity (m/s)}}{\text{time (s)}}$$

$$\text{(final velocity (m/s))}^2 - \text{(initial velocity (m/s))}^2 = 2 \times \text{acceleration (m/s}^2) \times \text{distance (m)}$$

- When an object is released close to the Earth's surface, it accelerates downwards.
- Then the acceleration is approximately 10m/s². This is called acceleration due to gravity, or acceleration of free fall, (g).

Quick Test

1. Calculate the kinetic energy, in joules (J), of a ball of mass 0.5kg moving at 16m/s.
2. Calculate how long a 100km journey would take at an average speed of 40kph.
3. Calculate the acceleration, in m/s², of a car that goes from standstill (0m/s) to 24m/s in 10s.
4. Suggest what the acceleration of a ball that is dropped to the ground would be.

Key Words

SI system
scalar quantity
kinetic energy
displacement
velocity
vector quantity
slope
gradient
acceleration
acceleration due to
    gravity (g)

Forces

You must be able to:

- Calculate combinations of forces that act along the same line
- Understand that forces act in pairs of the same size but opposite direction
- Recall that acceleration is not possible without net force, and a net force always produces acceleration.

Contact Force

- You can push and pull objects by making contact with them.
- The force you apply can be partly or completely a force of friction.
- Friction acts parallel to the surface of the object.
- You can also push at right-angles to the object. This is called a normal force.
- Force is measured in newtons, N.

Key Point

Force is a vector quantity – direction matters. Arrows can be drawn to show forces.

Non-Contact Force

- Two magnets can attract or repel each other without touching.
- Electric force also acts without contact (without touching).
- Gravity provides another force that can act at a distance.

Gravitational and Electric Force

- All objects that have mass experience gravitational force.
- All objects with electric charge experience electric force.
- Gravitational force is always attractive, so there must be only one kind of mass.
- The Earth attracts you. The force, measured in N, is your weight.
- Electric force can be attractive or repulsive, so there must be two kinds of electric charge – positive and negative.

Net Force

- The overall force for a combination of forces is called their resultant force or net force.
- When there is a net force on an object it *always* accelerates.
- When there is no force at all on an object or the forces are balanced, it *never* accelerates. (It can move, but the motion never changes.)
- A body stays still or keeps moving at constant velocity unless an external force acts on it. That idea is called Newton's first law.

Key Point

If net force is not zero, the forces are unbalanced and there is acceleration. If motion is steady and in a straight line, velocity is constant and there is no acceleration.

Direction of Force

- The direction of a force makes a big difference to the effect it has.
  - Two forces of the same size acting in opposite directions do *not* cause acceleration, so the net force is zero.
  - Two forces acting in the same direction add together to produce a bigger net force.
- When you push an object, you experience a force of the same size and in the opposite direction.

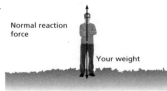

Normal reaction force

Your weight

- Newton's third law states that for every force there is an equal and opposite force.
- For example, a spacecraft can accelerate (or decelerate) by pushing gases (made by burning fuel) away from itself.
- When you stand on the floor:
  - your weight acts as a force on the floor
  - the floor provides an equal force in the opposite direction – this is called a normal reaction force.

Force and Acceleration

- Net force is related to acceleration in a fairly simple way:
  - acceleration is bigger when force is bigger
  - but smaller when mass is bigger.

> **force (N) = mass (kg) × acceleration (m/s²)**

- This equation is a form of Newton's second law.
- **HT** Mass of a body produces a resistance to acceleration when a force is applied to it. This resistance is inertia.

> **HT Key Point**
>
> The bigger the mass of an object, the greater the force needed to produce an acceleration. An object with more mass has more inertia, so it is more difficult to change its velocity.

HT Resistive Force on a Falling Object

- Air resistance creates a resistive force opposite to the force of gravity.
- The faster an object falls, the bigger the resistive force.
- Eventually the upwards resistive force becomes as big as the downwards gravitational force.
- The two forces are equal and opposite, so there is no net force.
- When there is no net force there is no acceleration, so a falling object continues to fall at constant velocity.
- That velocity is called the object's terminal velocity.

At first velocity is small so resistive force is small. There is a large net force acting downwards. The skydiver accelerates downwards.

As velocity increases, resistive force increases. But there is still a net downwards force so the skydiver continues to gain velocity.

Eventually, the velocity is so large that resistive force is the same size as the weight. Net force is zero. So acceleration is zero. Velocity stays the same.

> **Quick Test**
>
> 1. Name the kind of force that keeps you in your seat.
> 2. Name the kind of force that holds your body together.
> 3. State what is necessary, in terms of forces, for acceleration to happen.
> 4. **HT** When a ball is dropped, the effect of air resistance is ignored because it is so small. Explain why a skydiver, who jumps from a plane, cannot ignore the effect of air resistance.

> **Key Words**
>
> friction
> normal force
> repel
> resultant force
> net force
> external force
> Newton's first law
> Newton's third law
> Newton's second law
> **HT** resistive force
> **HT** terminal velocity

Force, Energy and Power

You must be able to:

- Select from a range of equations so that you can analyse and predict motion
- HT Understand what momentum is and that it is conserved in collisions
- Understand 'doing work' as mechanical energy transfer.

HT Momentum

- Momentum is the product of mass and velocity. It is a vector quantity, so direction is important.

> **momentum (kgm/s) = mass (kg) × velocity (m/s)**

- Whenever bodies collide, their total momentum is the same before and after the collision – it is conserved.

> **total momentum before = total momentum after**

Force, Work and Energy

- When a force acts and a body accelerates as a result of this force, energy is supplied to the body.
- We say that the force does work on the body.
- The amount of work done and the energy supplied to the body are the same:

> **work done (J) = energy supplied =**
> **force × distance (m) (along the line of action of the force)**

- The unit of energy is the joule (J).

> **1J = 1N × 1m**

- Work must be done to overcome friction as well as to cause acceleration.
- When there is friction, some or all of the energy causes heating.
- In some situations, some of the work done increases an object's potential energy.

> **(in a gravity field) potential energy (J) =**
> **mass (kg) × height (m) × gravitational field strength, g (N/kg)**

Energy Stores and Transfers

- Energy can be stored in different ways, e.g.
  - in the kinetic energy of a moving body
  - as gravitational potential energy
  - as elastic potential energy
  - as thermal energy.
- Energy can be taken from these stores and transferred to other systems.
- Sometimes the energy becomes thinly spread out and only heats the surroundings of a process. Then it cannot be usefully transferred.

> **energy transferred (J) = charge (C) × potential difference (V)**

- Wasted energy dissipates in the surroundings.

Power

- Energy can be transferred quickly or slowly.
- The rate of transfer of energy is power.

> **power (W) = rate of transfer of energy (J/s)**
> $$= \frac{\text{energy (J)}}{\text{time (s)}}$$

- Doing work is one way of transferring energy. It is energy transfer involving force and distance.
- So, when work is done:

 power (W) = $\frac{\text{work done (J)}}{\text{time (s)}}$

 Key Point

A bow and arrow, with the bowstring pulled back, is an example of an energy storage system. It's an elastic potential energy store.

Key Words

HT momentum
HT conserved
work
friction
potential energy
kinetic energy
gravitational potential energy
elastic potential energy
thermal energy
dissipate
power

Quick Test

1. HT Two balls of the same mass and with the same speed collide head on. State and explain what their total momentum is before the collision, and what their total momentum is after the collision.
2. An ice skater can move in a straight line at almost constant speed without needing to supply more energy. Explain, in terms of force and distance, how that is possible.
3. When you lean against a wall you are not doing work. Explain why in terms of force and distance.
4. Describe the relationship between power and energy.

Changes of Shape

You must be able to:

- Distinguish between plastic and elastic materials
- Distinguish between linear and non-linear relationships
- Understand that for a linear relationship, the slope or gradient is constant
- Recall that a planet's gravitational field strength depends on its mass.

Extension and Compression

- A pair of forces acting outwards on an object can stretch it, or **extend** it, even if the forces are balanced and there is no acceleration.
- A pair of forces acting inwards on an object can **compress** it.
- Combinations of forces can also bend objects.
- Change of shape can be called **deformation**.

Elastic and Plastic Deformation

- When forces make an object change shape, but it returns to its original shape when the forces are removed, the deformation is said to be **elastic**.
- If the object keeps its new shape when the deforming forces are removed, the deformation is **plastic**.

Extension of Springs

- A spring experiences elastic deformation unless the force applied is large. Then the spring may be permanently stretched.
- For a spring, unless the force is very large, the amount of extension is **proportional to** the size of the deforming force.
- When the force changes, the amount of the extension changes by the same proportion.
- A graph of extension and applied force is a straight line – the relationship between force and extension is **linear**.

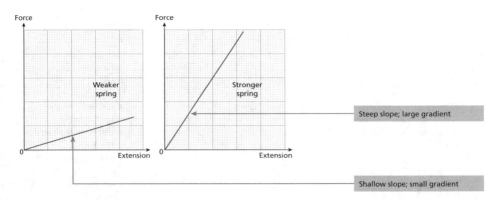

- The gradient of the graph is different for individual springs. It is called the spring constant.

 force exerted on a spring (N) =
extension (m) × spring constant (N/m)

- The graph produced by a rubber band is not a straight line. The relationship is non-linear.

Energy Stored by a Stretched Spring

- Stretching a spring involves force and distance (the extension) in the same direction. So work must be done to stretch a spring.

work done = average force × distance = $\left(\dfrac{\text{final force}}{2}\right)$ × distance

work done = energy transferred in stretching (J) =
0.5 × spring constant (N/m) × (extension (m))^2

Mass and Weight

- In Physics, we treat weight as a type of force, so we measure it in newtons (N). It is the force on an object due to gravity.
- Different planets and moons have different gravitational field strengths, g, at their surface. This means that objects have different weights on different planets and moons.
- Weight is related to mass:

weight = gravity force (N) =
mass (kg) × gravitational field strength, g (N/kg)

- On Earth, g = 10N/kg; on the Moon, g = 1.6N/kg; near the surface of Jupiter, g = 26N/kg.

Quick Test

1. A pair of forces that act on an object along the same line are balanced (equal size, opposite direction) and cannot accelerate the object. What effect can they have?
2. State which of the following show elastic behaviour and which show plastic behaviour:
   a) a guitar string
   b) a piece of modelling clay
   c) a saw blade when it is flicked
   d) a saw blade when a large force bends it permanently.
3. Physics distinguishes between mass and weight and uses different units (kg for mass and N for weight). Explain why this distinction is generally not used in everyday life.

Revise

 Key Words

extend
compress
deformation
elastic
plastic
proportional to
linear
spring constant
non-linear
weight
planet
moon
gravitational field
  strength (g)

Levers, Gears and Hydraulic Systems

You must be able to:

- Calculate the moment of a force and apply this to understanding levers
- Understand that for a balanced (non-rotating) object, total clockwise moments and total anticlockwise moments are equal
- Recall that a lever can multiply force but not energy
- Recall that gears and hydraulic systems can also multiply force.

Moments Around a Pivot

- Pairs of forces that act along different lines can make bodies rotate.
- A pivot can provide force.
- Another force, acting at a different point, can cause rotation around the pivot. This is an applied force.
- The turning effect of the applied force is called its moment.

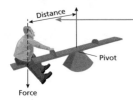

Distance

Pivot

Force

The bigger the distance from the pivot, the bigger the turning effect.

- The moment can be clockwise or anticlockwise around the pivot.
- The size of the moment depends on:
  - the force
  - the shortest distance from the line of the force to the pivot.

> **LEARN**
> moment of a force (Nm) =
> force (N) × distance (m) (normal to the direction of the force)

- The unit of moment is the newton-metre (Nm).
- This distance is at right-angles to the force.

Key Point

The turning effect of the applied force, relative to the pivot, is called its moment.

Balanced Objects

- If total clockwise moments and total anticlockwise moments are equal, the body is balanced.
- This is sometimes called the principle of moments.

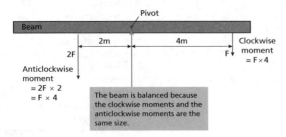

Pivot

Beam

2m

4m

2F

F

Clockwise moment
= F × 4

Anticlockwise moment
= 2F × 2
= F × 4

The beam is balanced because the clockwise moments and the anticlockwise moments are the same size.

Key Point

The principle of moments states that if a body is balanced the sum of the clockwise moments and the sum of the anticlockwise moments are in opposite direction and also equal in size.

Levers

- Because distance is important, a smaller force can 'beat' a bigger force.
- A lever can multiply the applied force to move a load, but the applied force must move through a bigger distance.
- A lever cannot multiply energy.

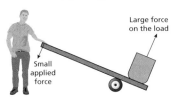

Large force on the load

Small applied force

Gears

- Gears can also use a smaller force to overcome a bigger force.
- If two cogs of different sizes are engaged together, the smaller cog makes more turns (or revolutions) for each turn of the bigger one.
- A small force applied to turn the smaller cog can act on a bigger load, through the bigger cog.

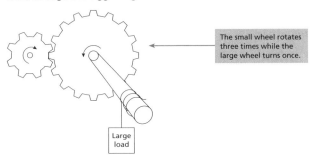

The small wheel rotates three times while the large wheel turns once.

Large load

A Hydraulic System

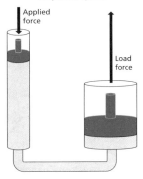

Applied force

Load force

Hydraulic Systems

- A hydraulic system can also multiply force.
- A hydraulic system – filled with liquid – can have a pair of pistons.
- A small force applied to a small piston with small area produces pressure, which is transmitted without reduction to a larger area.
- The force acting on a bigger piston is bigger than the applied force.

Key Words

rotate
pivot
applied force
moment
principle of moments
lever
multiply
load
gear
cog
hydraulic system
piston

Quick Test

1. Explain why a force acting at a pivot has no turning effect.
2. Outline the principle of moments.
3. Levers can multiply force (the applied force is smaller than the load). Explain why the point at which the force is applied must move through a larger distance than the load.
4. Use the relationship between force and pressure to explain how a hydraulic system multiplies force.

Review Questions

Electric Charge

1. Between which of these pairs of particles will there be a force of attraction?

   A (+)   (+)

   B Neutral (●)   (+)

   C Neutral (●)   (−)

   D (+)   (−)   [1]

2. Inside atoms, which particles have electric charge?

   A neutrons

   B neutrons and protons

   C neutrons, protons and electrons

   D protons and electrons   [1]

3. Why is it difficult to give a static charge to a metal object?

   A electrons can easily flow on and off the object

   B protons can easily flow on and off the object

   C there are no electrons in metals

   D electrons in metals can't move   [1]

4. What does the movement of many electrons in the same direction produce?

   A an electric charge

   B an electric current

   C an electric resistance   [1]

5 Which of these is a correct diagram of electric field lines?

A 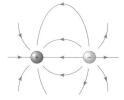   B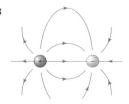

C 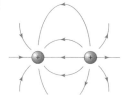   D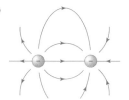

[1]

6 What is the unit of charge?

A amp

B coulomb

C joule

D volt

[1]

7 Which of these is a correct equation?

A current = charge × time

B current = $\dfrac{\text{charge}}{\text{time}}$

C charge = $\dfrac{\text{current}}{\text{time}}$

D time = current × charge

[1]

Total Marks .... / 7

Review Questions

Circuits

1 What component is this the symbol for?

[1]

2 Which of these will increase the current in a circuit?

    A increasing voltage and keeping resistance the same

    B increasing resistance and keeping voltage the same

    C decreasing voltage and keeping resistance the same

    D decreasing voltage and increasing resistance [1]

3 Explain:

    a) the difference between a volt (V) and a kilovolt (kV) [1]

    b) the difference between a cell and a battery [1]

    c) the difference between series and parallel connections [1]

    d) the difference between an ammeter and a voltmeter [1]

    e) the different ways in which ammeters and voltmeters are connected into circuits to investigate the current–voltage relationship for a component, such as a diode. [1]

4 **a)** Draw a circuit diagram for a circuit you would use to investigate the relationship between current and voltage for a filament lamp. [5]

    b) A filament lamp contains a wire that gets hot.

    Sketch a current–voltage graph for a filament lamp. [4]

    c) Explain why the graph in part **b)** is not perfectly straight. [2]

Total Marks _____ / 18

Resistors and Energy Transfers

1 Which of these pairs are both units of energy?

    A volt and joule

    B watt and joule

    C watt and kilowatt

    D joule and kilowatt-hour [1]

2 What happens to:

    a) the resistance of a thermistor when its temperature increases? [1]

    b) the resistance of an LDR when light level decreases? [1]

3 A kettle is rated at 2.0kW.

    a) Of what physical quantity is kW a unit? [1]

    b) During 1 week, the kettle is used for a total of 2.5 hours.

       How much energy does it transfer in the week? Give your answer in kWh. [3]

    c) The hour and the kWh are not SI units.

       What are the SI units for the same physical quantities? [2]

    d) Why are SI units not always used when working with appliances like kettles? [1]

    e) Repeat the calculation from part **b)**, this time using SI units. [2]

           Total Marks .... / 12

Practice Questions

Journeys

1. Which of these is **not** a unit of speed?

   A mph   B km/h   C m/s   D kg/s   [1]

2. How far can you walk in 3 hours at an average speed of 4km/h?

   A 0.75km   B 1.33km   C 7km   D 12km   [1]

3. Which of these is a unit of energy?

   A joule   B newton   C pascal   D watt   [1]

4. What happens to the speed of the Earth as it orbits the Sun?

   A it decreases

   B it stays the same

   C it increases

   D it changes direction   [1]

5. HT What happens to the velocity of the Earth as it orbits the Sun?

   A it decreases

   B it stays the same

   C it increases

   D it changes direction   [1]

6. How far can you travel in 1 hour at an average speed of:

   a) 24km/h?   [3]

   b) 40mph?   [2]

   c) 4m/s?   [3]

   d) i) Give your answer to part a) in metres.   [1]

      ii) Give your answer to part b) in metres.   [2]
          1mile = 1.6km = 1600m

7 Volume is a scalar quantity but force is a vector quantity.

    a) What is the difference between a vector and a scalar quantity? [1]

    b) Give another example of a vector quantity. [1]

    c) Give another example of a scalar quantity. [1]

8 A plane takes off in Hong Kong and lands in London 12 hours later. The distance of the journey is 6000km.

    a) What is its average speed in km/h? [2]

    b) What is its average speed in m/s? [2]

    c) HT For most of the flight, speed does not change much, but velocity does. [2]

       In what way does the velocity change?

9 HT A spaceship can keep travelling in a straight line without slowing down.

    a) Why can't a car do the same? [1]

    b) How does a spaceship accelerate? [1]

Total Marks _____ / 27

Forces

1 Which of these forces requires contact?

    A electric or electrostatic force

    B frictional force

    C gravitational force

    D magnetic force [1]

Practice Questions

2   Which graph shows acceleration?

A

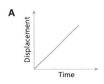

C

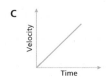

B

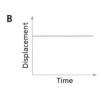

D

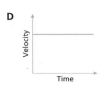

[1]

3   HT What always produces resistance to acceleration?

     A   energy   **B**   mass   **C**   pressure   **D**   velocity   [1]

4   If a ball is kicked along the ground it eventually slows down and stops, i.e. it decelerates.

     What force causes this deceleration?   [1]

5   What does Newton's first law say about force?   [1]

6   What does Newton's third law say about force?   [1]

> **Total Marks** _____ / 6

Force, Energy and Power

1   Which of these is necessary for doing work?

     A   energy   **B**   mass   **C**   pressure   **D**   velocity   [1]

2   If the point of a pin has an area of $1 \times 10^{-7} m^2$, how much pressure does it exert
     on a surface when it is pushed with a force of 10N?

     A $10^{-8}Pa$ **B** $10^{-6}Pa$ **C** $10^{6}Pa$ **D** $10^{8}Pa$ [1]

> **Total Marks** _____ / 2

Changes of Shape

1 What word describes the behaviour of a material that keeps its new shape after a deforming force is removed?

  A elastic

  B plastic

  C compressed

  D extended [1]

2 Here are four force-extension graphs, with the same scales on both axes, for four different springs.

Which graph has the biggest spring constant?

A

C

B

D

[1]

3 In physics, which is the correct statement about weight?

  A Weight is a quantity measured in kilograms (kg).

  B Weight is a quantity measured in joules (J).

  C Weight is the force of gravity.

  D Weight is the gravitational field strength. [1]

Total Marks .... / 3

Practice Questions

Levers, Gears and Hydraulic Systems

1 What is the turning effect of a force called?

    A moment

    B pivot

    C pressure

    D work [1]

2 What is a hydraulic system filled with?

    A gas because it transmits pressure

    B gas because it doesn't transmit pressure

    C liquid because it transmits pressure

    D liquid because it doesn't transmit pressure [1]

3 **a)** What is the moment of a force of 18N that acts 1.5m from a pivot? [3]

    b) If this force is the applied force acting on a lever, what will be the force that acts
    on a load placed 0.3m from the pivot? [3]

4 Describe the effects of the forces on the beam in each of the following examples:

    a)

[1]

    b)

[1]

    c)

[1]

Total Marks .... / 11

Journeys

1 What is 100 miles in kilometres?

$$\frac{1 \text{ mile}}{1 \text{ kilometre}} = \frac{8}{5}$$

    A 160km   **B** 62.5km   **C** 60km   **D** 21.6km   [1]

2 How far can you walk in 2.5 hours at an average speed of 1m/s?

    A 1440m   **B** 9000m   **C** 10800m   **D** 12600m   [1]

3 Which of these is the fastest speed?

$$\frac{1 \text{ mile}}{1 \text{ kilometre}} = \frac{8}{5}$$

    A 36km/h   **C** 10m/s

    B 36000m/h   **D** 25mph   [1]

4 Which graph shows constant velocity?

A Displacement

C Velocity

B Displacement

D Velocity
    [1]

5 A car is travelling at 5m/s and then speeds up to 15m/s. It takes 10s to do this.

What is the car's acceleration?

    A 0.5m/s^2 **B** 1m/s^2 **C** 2m/s^2 **D** 10m/s^2 [1]

Review Questions

6 The diagram shows the velocity vectors of a car at two times, T_1 and T_2, one minute apart.

T_1 T_2

a) What has happened to the speed of the car? [1]

b) What has happened to the velocity of the car? [1]

c) Has the car accelerated or decelerated? [1]

d) What can you say about the force acting on the car? [1]

7 **a)** A sports car can accelerate from standstill (velocity = 0) to 30m/s in 10s.

   What is its acceleration? [3]

b) If the mass of the car is 1000kg, what is its kinetic energy:

   i) when it is standing still? [1]

   ii) when it is moving at 30m/s? [3]

c) What average force is needed to accelerate the car? [3]

d) Use the following equation
   (final velocity (m/s))^2 – (initial velocity (m/s))^2 = 2 × acceleration (m/s^2) × distance (m)
   to work out the distance the car travels during this acceleration. [2]

e) Calculate the amount of work that is needed for the car's acceleration. [3]

f) What is the power at which the car gains energy? [2]

Total Marks _____ / 26

Forces

1. What type of force acts on the Earth to keep it in orbit?

   A electric or electrostatic force   **C** magnetic force

   B gravitational force   **D** resistive force   [1]

2. Which of these always causes acceleration?

   A unbalanced or net force   **C** constant velocity

   B balanced forces   **D** constant pressure   [1]

3. How much force is needed to accelerate a mass of 20kg by 4m/s²?

   A 5N   **B** 16N   **C** 24N   **D** 80N   [1]

4. **a)** When a person steps off a boat, what does their foot do to the boat?   [1]

   b) What happens to the boat:

      i) if it is much more massive than the person?   [1]

      ii) if it is not much more massive than the person?   [1]

   c) Sketch the forces acting on the person and on the boat.   [3]

5. Humans cannot jump very high.

   Why not?   [1]

6. Describe the net force or resultant force for each of the following examples.

   a)   [1]

   b)   [1]

   c)   [1]

Total Marks .... / 13

Review Questions

Force, Energy and Power

1 What is power the same as?

    A change of momentum   **C** rate of energy transfer

    B kinetic energy   **D** strength   [1]

2 A person has to do work to push a cupboard across a room.

    a) If they push it for 2.5m with an average force of 180N, how much work do they do?   [3]

    b) If the cupboard is floating in space, and it experiences a force of 180N over a distance of 2.5m, how much kinetic energy does it gain?   [1]

    c) Why doesn't the cupboard in the room gain kinetic energy?   [1]

    d) On Earth, imagine that the cupboard experiences an **upwards** force equal to its weight, 300N, and rises steadily to a height of 2.5m.

    What can you say about the cupboard's energy?   [3]

> **Total Marks** _____ / 9

Changes of Shape

1 Which of the following best describes the relationship between force and extension for an elastic spring?

    A constant   **B** linear   **C** non-linear   **D** varying   [1]

2 **a)** What is the weight on Earth, in newtons (N), of a ball with mass of 1.2kg?   [3]

    b) If g_{moon} and $g_{jupiter}$ are 1.6N/kg and 25N/kg, how much will the ball weigh on **i)** the Moon and **ii)** on Jupiter?   [2]

> **Total Marks** _____ / 6

Levers, Gears and Hydraulic Systems

1 Complete the sentence.

A lever is a force multiplier. This means that:

A the applied force is bigger than the load force and moves further.

B the applied force is bigger than the load force and doesn't move so far.

C the load force is bigger than the applied force and moves further.

D the load force is bigger than the applied force and doesn't move so far. [1]

2 Which of these diagrams accurately shows a lever being used to lift a load? [1]

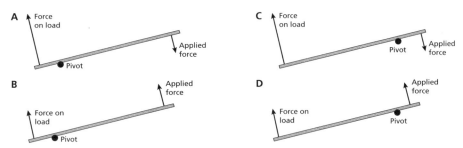

3 A force of 180N is made to act on a movable piston of a hydraulic system.
The area of the piston is 0.2m².
The system has a second moveable piston with an area of 0.8m².

a) What is the pressure inside the system? [3]

b) How much force acts at the second piston? [3]

c) What is the use of a hydraulic system like this? [1]

4 A child with weight 30kg sits 1.5m from the pivot of a seesaw.

Calculate where another child should sit to balance the seesaw, if she has a weight of 20kg. [3]

Total Marks _____ / 12

Answers

Page 5 Quick Test
1. Electric force can be attractive or repulsive.
2. a) Electrons are transferred to or from the surface by friction.
   b) Electrons can flow within the metal, and even our skin can conduct some electricity. So when we hold the spoon, charge can flow to or from it and it doesn't stay charged.
3. Current is rate of flow of charge.
4. Current through resistance causes heating, so the surroundings are heated.

Page 7 Quick Test
1. A voltmeter measures the potential difference between two points.
2. a) An increase in voltage, or a decrease in resistance
   b) A decrease in voltage, or an increase in resistance
3. resistance $= \dfrac{\text{voltage}}{\text{current}}$. A metal wire's resistance increases when it is hot, so the ratio of voltage to current increases.
4. It decreases.

Page 9 Quick Test
1. a) total resistance $= 2 + 4$
   $= 6\Omega$
   b) $\dfrac{1}{\text{total resistance}} = \dfrac{1}{2} + \dfrac{1}{4}$
   $= \dfrac{3}{4}$
   total resistance $= \dfrac{4}{3}$
   $= 1.33\Omega$
2. They transfer energy by doing work (= force × distance) on objects outside the circuit, such as by lifting loads. (They may also become warm, and transfer some energy to the surroundings by heating.)
3. a) energy transfer =
   current × voltage × time
   $= 1.5 \times 12 \times 60$
   $= 1080J$
   b) power = current × voltage
   $= 1.5 \times 12$
   $= 18W$
   OR
   power $= \dfrac{\text{energy}}{\text{time}}$
   $= \dfrac{1080}{60}$
   $= 18W$

Page 10 Electric charge
1. C [1]
2. C [1]
3. B [1]
4. C [1]

5. a) There are two kinds (negative and positive) [1]
   b) Two bodies with unlike charges [1]
   c) Two bodies with like charges [1]
6. a) Metals have electrons that are free to move, they are not all attached to individual atoms [1]
   b) Resistors resist the flow of electrons, so kinetic energy is transferred from the electrons [1]; resulting in an increase in temperature [1]

Remember that resistors are energy transfer devices. They transfer energy out from a circuit by heating the surroundings. The energy then usually spreads into the surroundings, or dissipates.

   c) Some current can pass through each of the resistors [1]

Page 11 Circuits
1. D [1]
2. B [1]
3. C [1]
4. A [1]
5. A [1]
6. B [1]
7. D [1]
8. a) The cells are opposing each other [1]
   b) The diodes are opposing each other [1]
   c) The voltmeter is connected in series but should be in parallel [1]
   d) The positions of the switches mean that there is not a complete circuit [1]
9. a) To supply energy / create a potential difference or voltage [1]
   b) To measure current [1]
   c) To measure voltage / potential difference [1]
   d) To oppose current / to control current (or voltage) / or to provide heating [1]
   e) To allow current in only one direction [1]
   f) To change current (or voltage), depending on temperature [1]
   g) To change current (or voltage) [1], depending on light brightness [1]
10. a) voltage = current × resistance [1];
    $= 1.5 \times 6$ [1];
    $= 9V$ [1]
   b) charge moved = current × time [1];
    $= 1.5 \times 60$ [1];
    $= 90C$ [1]
   c) energy transferred =
    current × voltage × time [1];
    $= 1.5 \times 9 \times 60$ [1];
    $= 810J$ [1]
   d) rate of transfer of energy
    = power
    $= \dfrac{\text{energy}}{\text{time}}$ [1];
    $= \dfrac{810}{60}$ [1];
    $= 13.5W$ [1]

OR
    = current × voltage [1];
    $= 1.5 \times 9$ [1];
    $= 13.5W$ [1]

Remember, units matter – never forget to include the unit with your answer.

Page 13 Resistors and Energy Transfers
1. B [1]

Page 15 Quick Test
1. kinetic energy = 0.5 × mass and speed^2
   $= 0.5 \times 0.5 \times 16^2$
   $= 64J$

Do calculations like these step-by-step. Always start by writing the equation. Then put in the numbers. Do the arithmetic and don't forget to write the final unit. If you try to do everything all at once you'll often get confused and make mistakes.

2. time $= \dfrac{\text{distance}}{\text{speed}}$
   $= \dfrac{100}{40}$
   $= 2.5$ hours
3. acceleration $= \dfrac{\text{change in velocity}}{\text{time}}$
   $= \dfrac{(24-0)}{10}$
   $= 2.4m/s^2$
4. $10m/s^2$, which is the acceleration of free fall

Page 17 Quick Test
1. Gravity, or gravitational force (i.e. weight)
2. Electric or electrical force
3. Unbalanced (or net or resultant) force

Remember that unbalanced force **always** causes acceleration of a body.

4. The skydiver falls a long distance and accelerates to high velocity. Resistive force increases as velocity increases. (Also, the surface area of the skydiver is large enough that the air resistance is substantial.)

Page 19 Quick Test
1. Zero and zero.

The two balls have the same mass and the same speed. Because they are traveling in opposite directions, their momentums cancel each other out – the total is zero.

2. The ice skater experiences low resistive force (friction) so loses little energy, and needs to do little work to replace lost energy.
3. A person leaning on a wall exerts a force on it, but the wall doesn't move and there is no distance involved. Work = force × distance = force × 0 = 0.
4. Power is rate of transferring energy / power measures how quickly energy is transferred.

Page 21 Quick Test
1. They can change its shape / cause extension or compression.

   If the forces acting on a body are balanced then there can be no acceleration, but shape can change and this can be extension or compression.

2. a) elastic
   b) plastic
   c) elastic
   d) plastic
3. Physics concerns the whole universe, and weight for an equivalent mass is very different in different places. On the Earth's surface, the weight of a particular mass is much the same everywhere so the distinction is not relevant.

Page 23 Quick Test
1. Turning effect or moment = force × shortest distance. The distance between the force and the pivot is zero.
2. An object will be balanced when total clockwise moments are equal to total anticlockwise moments.
3. Levers can't multiply energy. The work done on the load can't be more than work done by the applied force. Work is force × distance, so if force on the load is increased by the lever then the distance moved by the load must be smaller.

   The load cannot gain more energy than is supplied to the lever. It's an example of conservation of energy.

4. pressure = $\frac{force}{area}$, so
   force = pressure × area. If pressure is the same but area is bigger, then force is bigger.

Page 24 Electric charge
1. D [1]
2. D [1]
3. A [1]
4. B [1]
5. B [1]
6. B [1]
7. B [1]

Page 26 Circuits
1. A diode [1]
2. A [1]
3. a) A kilovolt is 1000 volts. [1]
   b) A battery has more than one cell. [1]
   c) In series circuits the current passes through one component after another, but in a parallel circuit it passes through one or the other / the current divides. [1]
   d) An ammeter measures current; a voltmeter measures voltage or potential difference. [1]
   e) The ammeter is connected in series with the component; the voltmeter is connected across it, in parallel with it. [1]
4. a) Circuit drawn with: cell or battery and switch [1]; ammeter [1]; filament lamp [1]; the components all in a series [1]; voltmeter in parallel with the lamp [1]

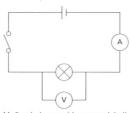

   b) Graph drawn with: current labelled on y-axis [1]; voltage labelled on x-axis [1]; line is straight at low current [1]; line becomes curved, towards the voltage axis [1]

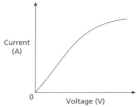

Current (A)

0   Voltage (V)

   c) Resistance is higher when the wire is hot [1]; due to increased difficulty of electron flow [1]

Page 27 Resistors and Energy Transfers
1. D [1]
2. a) It decreases [1]
   b) It increases [1]
3. a) Power [1]
   b) energy = power × time [1];
      = 2 × 2.5 [1];
      = 5kWh [1]

   Remember that the kilowatt-hour, kWh, is a unit of energy but the kilowatt, kW, is a unit of power.

   c) Second [1]; joule [1]
   d) The SI units are small [1]
   e) energy = power × time
      = 2000 × 2.5 × 3600 [1];
      = 18 000 000J or 1.8 × 10^{7}J [1]

Page 28 Journeys
1. D [1]
2. D [1]
3. A [1]
4. B [1]
5. D [1]
6. a) distance = speed × time [1];
      = 24 [1]; kilometres [1]
   b) distance = speed × time
      = 40 [1]; miles [1]
   c) distance = speed × time
      = 4 [1]; × 3600 [1];
      = 14400m [1]

   There are 60 × 60 = 3600 seconds in an hour.

   d) i) 24 000m [1]
      ii) 40 × 1600 [1]; = 64 000m [1]
7. a) A scalar has size, a vector has size and direction [1]
   b) Any one from: displacement [1]; force [1]; velocity [1]; acceleration [1] ; momentum [1]
   c) Any one from: energy [1]; distance [1]; area [1]; speed [1]
8. a) speed = $\frac{distance}{time}$ [1];
      = $\frac{6000}{12}$ [1];
      = 500km/h [1]
   b) 500 × $\frac{1000}{3600}$ [1]; =139m/s [1]
   c) Direction changes [1]; including change due to curvature of the Earth [1]
9. a) The car experiences resistive forces [1]
   b) It projects material (gas), in the opposite direction to the acceleration / backwards [1]

Page 29 Forces
1. B [1]
2. C [1]
3. B [1]
4. Friction / resistive force [1]
5. A body can't accelerate without force / the acceleration of a body is proportional to the resultant force acting on it / force = mass × acceleration [1]
6. Any body that exerts a force on another itself experiences an equal force in the opposite direction [1]

Page 30 Force, Energy and Power
1. A [1]
2. D [1]

Answers

Page 31 Changes of Shape
1. B [1]
2. A [1]
3. C [1]

Page 32 Levers, Gears and Hydraulic Systems
1. A [1]
2. C [1]
3. a) moment = force × distance [1];
   = 18 × 1.5 [1];
   = 27Nm [1]

   b) force = $\dfrac{\text{moment}}{\text{distance}}$ [1];

   = $\dfrac{27}{0.3}$ (or similar working) [1];

   = 90N [1]
4. a) Balance [1]
   b) Rotation, anticlockwise [1]
   c) No (turning) effect [1]

Pages 33–37 Review Questions

Page 33 Journeys
1. A [1]
2. B [1]
3. D [1]
4. A [1]
5. B [1]
6. a) It has decreased [1]
   b) It has decreased and changed direction [1]
   c) Decelerated [1]
   d) It is a braking / resistive force [1]

7. a) acceleration = $\dfrac{\text{change in speed}}{\text{time}}$ [1];

   = $\dfrac{30}{10}$ [1];

   = 3m/s^2 [1]

   b) i) 0 [1]
   ii) kinetic energy =
      0.5 × mass × speed^2 [1];
      = 0.5 × 1000 × 30^2 [1];
      = 450 000J or 450kJ [1]

   c) force = mass × acceleration [1];
      = 1000 × 3 [1];
      = 3000N [1]

   d) distance = $\dfrac{(30^2 - 0)}{(2 \times 3)}$ [1];

      = 150m [1]

   e) work done = force × distance [1];
      = (3000 × 150) [1];
      = 450 000J or 450kJ [1]

   f) power = $\dfrac{\text{energy or work}}{\text{time}}$ [1];

      = 45 000W or 45kW [1]

Page 35 Forces
1. B [1]
2. A [1]
3. D [1]

4. a) Pushes / exerts a force [1]
   b) i) little effect [1]
      ii) it accelerates / moves [1]
   c) **Diagram to show:** forces of the same size [1]; opposite directions [1]; acting on person and boat [1]

5. Gravity is too strong / weight is too big [1]
6. a) Large force to the right [1]
   b) Smaller force than answer a to the right [1]
   c) No net force [1]

Page 36 Force, Energy and Power
1. C [1]
2. a) work = force × distance [1];
      = 180 × 2.5 [1];
      = 450J [1]
   b) 450J [1]
   c) Because of resistive forces / friction [1]
   d) It gains gravitational potential energy [1]; of 300 × 2.5 [1] = 750 J [1]

Page 36 Changes of Shape
1. B [1]
2. a) weight = mass × g [1];
      = 1.2 × 10 [1];
      = 12N [1]
   b) i) 1.9(2)N on the Moon [1]
      ii) 30N on Jupiter [1]

Page 37 Levers, Gears and Hydraulic Systems
1. D [1]
2. A [1]
3. a) pressure = $\dfrac{\text{force}}{\text{area}}$ [1];

   = $\dfrac{180}{0.2}$ [1];

   = 900Pa [1]

   b) force = pressure × area [1];
      = 900 × 0.8 [1];
      = 720N [1]
   c) A small applied force can move a larger load / it multiplies force [1]
4. clockwise moments = anticlockwise moments [1];
   300 × 1.5 = 200 × distance [1];
   distance = 2.25m [1]

Physics Equations

You must be able to recall and apply the following equations using the appropriate SI units:

Word Equation
density (kg/m³) = $\dfrac{\text{mass (kg)}}{\text{volume (m}^3\text{)}}$
distance travelled (m) = speed (m/s) × time (s)
acceleration (m/s²) = $\dfrac{\text{change in velocity (m/s)}}{\text{time (s)}}$
kinetic energy (J) = 0.5 × mass (kg) × (speed (m/s))²
force (N) = mass (kg) × acceleration (m/s²)
 HT momentum (kgm/s) = mass (kg) × velocity (m/s)
work done (J) = force (N) × distance (m) (along the line of action of the force)
power (W) = $\dfrac{\text{work done (J)}}{\text{time (s)}}$
force exerted by a spring (N) = extension (m) × spring constant (N/m)
gravity force (N) = mass (kg) × gravitational field strength, g (N/kg)
(in a gravity field) potential energy (J) = mass (kg) × height (m) × gravitational field strength, g (N/kg)
pressure (Pa) = $\dfrac{\text{force normal to a surface (N)}}{\text{area of that surface (m}^2\text{)}}$
moment of a force (Nm) = force (N) × distance (m) (normal to direction of the force)
charge flow (C) = current (A) × time (s)
potential difference (V) = current (A) × resistance (Ω)
energy transferred (J) = charge (C) × potential difference (V)
power (W) = potential difference (V) × current (A) = (current (A))² × resistance (Ω)
energy transferred (J, kWh) = power (W, kW) × time (s, h)
wave speed (m/s) = frequency (Hz) × wavelength (m)
efficiency = $\dfrac{\text{useful output energy transfer (J)}}{\text{input energy transfer (J)}}$ × 100%

Physics Equations

You must be able to select and apply the following equations using the appropriate SI units:

Word Equation
change in thermal energy (J) = mass (kg) × specific heat capacity (J/kg°C) × change in temperature (°C)
thermal energy for a change in state (J) = mass (kg) × specific latent heat (J/kg)
(for gases) pressure (Pa) × volume (m³) = constant (for a given mass of gas at a constant temperature)
HT pressure due to a column of liquid (Pa) = height of column (m) × density of liquid (kg/m³) × g (N/kg)
(final velocity (m/s))² – (initial velocity (m/s))² = 2 × acceleration (m/s²) × distance (m)
energy transferred in stretching (J) = 0.5 × spring constant (N/m) × (extension (m))²
HT force on a conductor (at right-angles to a magnetic field) carrying a current (N) = magnetic field strength (T) × current (A) × length (m)
HT $\dfrac{\text{potential difference across primary coil (V)}}{\text{potential difference across secondary coil (V)}} = \dfrac{\text{number of turns in primary coil}}{\text{number of turns in secondary coil}}$
potential difference across primary coil (V) × current in primary coil (A) = potential difference across secondary coil (V) × current in secondary coil (A)

Notes

Notes

Notes